DESIGN

The Colorado Prize
David Milofsky, Series Editor

DESIGN

Sally Keith

Center *for* Literary Publishing
Fort Collins

Set in Adobe Garamond.
Printed in the United States of America by Maple-Vail.
Cover designed by Matt Williamson.

Library of Congress
Cataloging-in-Publication Data

Keith, Sally.
    Design / by Sally Keith.
    p.   cm.
    "Winner of the Colorado Prize for Poetry."
    ISBN 0-87081-603-9 (pbk.: alk.paper)
    I. Title

    PS3561.E3773 D4 2000
    811'.6—dc21   00-031703

The paper used in this book meets the minimum
requirements of the American National Standard
for Information Sciences—Permanence of Paper
for Printed Library Materials, ANSI Z39.48-1984.

1 2 3 4 5 04 03 02 01 00

For my mother and father
and for Maria, Hannah, and Jimmy

CONTENTS

FOREWORD

If ritual was feeding, who would refuse the feast?
—Sally Keith, "In Winter"

A good poet delivers new knowledge. I am happy to introduce Sally Keith because she does just that. What does *new* mean when we speak of new poetry—and of Sally Keith's *Design* in particular?

There is a poetry of the "infinite past" (D. H. Lawrence's expression) and of the "infinite future," a poetry of the "what has been" or the "to come." But despite the boasts of tradition (Hesiod, Yeats), there is no poetry of that "passing" *in which we dwell* (except in elegiac retrospect or petitional prospect). Language itself by its otherness to the world of reference, its very power, seems to block our engagement with what happens to us.

Sally Keith's book intends to contribute by poetic means—and does contribute—a powerful account of experience (precisely the *erlebnis*, experience *itself* so hard to encounter) of which the tradition gives no account. Keith focuses attention on those poetic aspects of language that make poetic language different from the language of category and reference; that is to say, her poetry undertakes to supply something that is inevitable in experience and nonetheless both "new" in expression and utterly appropriate to poetic expression:

> Do not make me
>   a middle thing
> I remember you
>   here—
>
> it stains my hands all day
>   ("Corymb")

By removing her poet from the "middle," Sally Keith also dispenses with the poetic interventions that defer experience. There are no holidays here, only calendric numbers specifying experiential instances. No festivals, only dates, as in Celan. No conventional forms, only line, the mere theater of breath and meaning.

Keith's text intends to convey—and does convey—a vertiginous sense of the otherwise unimaginable proximity of the world, not looking down from a great lyric height, or back from an elegiac distance of unrecoverability, or panegyric abjection, or petitional lack: but in the rich disorientation of an utterly lucid discourse of the at-handness of persons and things of which no one, or almost no one, has ever spoken, she "unravel[s] the black veil's hue. We emerge" ("Design").

The boldness of poetry of this kind (the great moral interest of Keith's book and project) is exemplified by its contradiction of the strange (prevalent and mistaken) poetic realism that insists we are forever separated from the experience that supplies our meaningful life. The pre-Socratics (Herakleitus) contributed the observation that we never can step in the same stream twice. Hence we have it on authority that there is no experience. Sally Keith's *Design* returns us to the proper business of poetry (*a new realism*) by her declaration (the theme of her *Design*) in context of the simplest of questions and the hard (but simple) answer

> *Will you*
> > *not come again?*
> I will cross—
> the river twice.
> > ("Mechanics")

ALLEN GROSSMAN

ACKNOWLEDGMENTS

Grateful acknowledgment is made to the editors of the following journals, in which some of these poems first appeared: *American Letters & Commentary, Colorado Review, Web Conjunctions, Field, Iowa Journal of Cultural Studies, Quarterly West, Ohio Review, Phoebe, Sonora Review,* and *Volt.*

I thank Allen Grossman and the Center for Literary Publishing.

Further gratitude to my teachers, especially Cynthia Hogue, Carolyn Forché, Jorie Graham, Mark Levine, James Galvin, and Susan Wheeler; the Breadloaf Writers' Conference; my peers at Iowa, particularly, and with great admiration, to Dan.

ONE

CORYMB

Milkweed-silk
    curled frond
        gray fell
longing
      spins

an arm's-length
    one grasping
        each stem
carrying
      its heavy bud—

turning fern-fronds
    examining near-white
        paled-green
asks texture
      our language

bolt-in spores
    clamping thin
        silence
the closed throat
      flowerless

without seed
    root and stem and frond
        a dell
thick with words
      unspoken

*

Shingled-roof
    the rut of math
        my rock rolls down
rough chutes
        bent jumps

propulsion leers
    branching speed
        hurdling notches
this crying is slow
        against it

the voice ricochets
    or soft
        —so caught
marble in a curve
        and plangent

questions
    pulling color out
        pulling grayed-
green out
        each still spire

and the sky
    carried down on wind
        plaintive curve
what ekes
        from the fell?

*

Where was I?
> *O my floating life—*
>> what place, what
need
> to be named—

milkweed
> how did I keep
>> forgotten colors
still
> knotted soft—

my curious—why
> fingers
>> separate strands
to find
> sleek-bodied seeds

buried
> I am lost with speed
>> —consciousness
the sudden
> silken-grit

inside
> Do not make me
>> a middle-thing
I remember you
> here—

it stains my hands all day

IN WINTER

Underneath, I understand—

    spend all morning watching wing-span, watching
birds drop down, turkey vultures circling, waiting
      to fall. And the body's color is distinguished
from the wings. This lightness pulled, in flight.
    I think the body is a spanning, a T.

But my eye is unable. Cannot say. For example, where

    does the inward breath end?
  The smokestacks (here) are vertical.
    The smokestacks (here) are black
or brown. The snow is white. The roofs fall down.
    And the voice (here). What does it mean?

Do you believe the way a bird falls depends on wind?

    The movement (now) is massed, a swallowing—
a flitting. These shrieking grackles fall in fury
      to the field. And the tangling (now) is light.
And whose is the field? And do the layers have laws?
    Do the birds fall faster closer to the ground?

The grackles' wings on winter wheat glint a silver blue.

    And there is a space (soft sibilance
in flight) I cannot see. This winter skill is uncanny
    overlapping stroke-lengths, white
or gray, in expectation of some end. I understand if—
    the lines behind the magpie mimic the yellowing sky.

These visions are all in winter.

The hymn explains all the world as God's own field.

    But if asked (and I fear) that I be
sifted like wheat, I too well know—
    I will not stumble, but give in. And what—
would you say? Why would you say it three times?

If the ritual were feeding, who would refuse the feast?

    It reminds me: I do not know winter.
Do the leaves completely fall? The vine creeps red
    on a white wall. Can you predict this? Winter
wheat, bright green. Berries blue or berries red.

Is there enough space here for a voice?

    Assuredly, my hands
are unable. Nature is composition. As the tide
    comes in, the creek digs back
into the softened shore. And further up the bight

we see the wind stop, the lines (on water) disappear.

    The dead leaves float beneath the dock, their shadows
pinned a pace behind. A hornet's nest (color: sand) connects
    the corner. And (on the outside) the wood is painted
white. Is chipping. And (inside) the boat is gone.

But absence says nothing. Again,

    I do not understand. I do not want to hear it,
three times. The space is too small. The boat
    is gone. My eyes unable. My hands—
do not speak. I do not. What is composition?

Why does the single branch so neatly fall?

* * *

One black mass crowns the upper edge of three

bare trees. The shrieking is too far away to hear.

It is a shifting in the wind. The birds have given

the branches weight. The leaves (left) are tin.

DESIGN

Leave me in the wind, numb—
    biting cries, gusts

tearing lines into the colorless
        sky. Fold me—the rough

crinoline, thickening night's numbers.
    Let the squalls dig
    deeper and heavier sounds fall.

How can the body keep?

Lament: the tightly curved back. Leave me
    filling myself with residue, soaking

accordion notes left in dusk's light. I'm counting
        the echoing notches of wind.

Doors slam. Or: wind lifts. Here, the tunnel
    length. I am shaking—

What is dust if the ground is

    hard, or trodden, so—which surface is wall?
It hangs on me like shoulders.
                I cannot

      lift my swollen feet, nor free them
    this stagnant river weighs.

Without wind, description saying nothing.

Even blue skies our mind shrouds
      pushing the tunnel further

    unraveling the black veil's hue. We emerge.
And how do I move? How

                                    can I
                        lift a single foot into this field?

                                    * * *

Departing, sculpture was a body, or—

     What was the figure sunken in lead?
Three photographs—four open doors
                                    the shadows

     trapezoids thrown on cold floor, one body
(I will not remember the whole), but the leaden edge—

          I know the blackness jutted
     from the wall. The photographs are gone.

The search dissipates.

     But dented black on a white wall. Could we
               have touched it? Would our hands

          remember it? I know, I watched it
too long, moved the lens too close,

     hoping to catch it

some intricacy, I cannot remember—

          The doors swing through me
     framing small medleys of wind in my chest.

The heart becomes
                    obscure, forgot—
     valves, chambers

circulation depends on this certain space
          I've learned it—
                    I've forgot—

          The depth of the river (mute, this heavy tongue
     caught in my throat) no severed whistle

                                    10

of wind, no roping water to polish
                the riverbed's rock. Ironclad

   the heart. Unframed. The vase too delicate
                       for forsythia's early sticks.

Find me my photograph of doors.

   The ear against a chest will hear
              the subtle murmur of each breath

the sound last words make, pressing up whole
   from the fallen mouth, the lingering hum

can't stop. These words can't last—
only their hard shapes, made to carry

           the body's final weight.
Leave me. The river is moving too fast.

                  * * *

   This woman sketches to speak—an empty chair,
a doorway, my halved face soaking in the dark.

     Why does this image last? Charcoal
bleeds. The river digs. I, still, can't sleep.

She gives me the sketch, explaining
                    departure—
Leave me.

I can't remember the leaden body's shape, sculpted on the wall.

   I have kept one photograph. Remember.
   The hair. The hands. How her black shirt

   hung. I can say one name. I know. I stood.
   I stand, alone. Two hands on one wall.

The river has disappeared, unscrewed
time's hinge. And yellow, the grass grows.

Worn stones in the riverbed. Weight
lines my arms. I'm gathering.

ENTRY

I

At sunset deep pallor if sun's lingered longer
    there, filtered blinds or glazed
paint, finishing wood floors. It soaks bedposts
    sorts shadow from door.

Note: Gaunt is a thinness come from suffering.

Through the north-facing window: a field.
    Paint between panes, chipping
off red. Mulberry. Dogwood berries
    of late summer—the subtle thief
lingering, leaving—

Note that: Lingering coming from light is green.

Where one field was plowed feet sunk in. What shined?
    Where one field was harvested
the next was not. What stopped? Beginning—
    exposed ground, middle—hay, then—
then the rising, the blue.

Note: The house comes back in narrow rays, thin wood.

Again, looking out. But the field?—
    Looking closer now. The strewn
hay feels. Sharp. Where it lies random, between
    careful rows. Meaning makes vision magnified.

That: One body comes as shoulder blades moving a back.

Note: Fields more ocean than stream.

Turquoise water. Touching elbows quick,
    staring down long. Losing sight watching
    color roil, hearing water's moiling

lapse from the pebbled shore. Further, fields
    torque color, terra shades. The variants—
    the twisting of greens: physical difference.

Breath slips, the green I'd held slips—
    falls to dull brown; the eye's clench—

Note that: We cannot see ourselves as landscape. We are.

3

Note: I am alone.

No grotto. No place of smooth. Late afternoon—
    the pieces of light are very exact. Hands,
my hands on a textured wall. Silence
    swarms, black. Seeps—thick. What is
an open wall? Has this shifting been
    exact? *Can you see me against the open
sky?* The throng of silence is a calling.
    Do I repulse it, keep straining away or fall?

NOTE: 03 FEBRUARY

*

One dark sun's rising
leaves no silhouette.
Alone—I

watch (the shadow takes
the face away) words
stir up from dust.

An aggregate (we are
blinded)—of spores
shifts quick

with wind. Pruned—
I pine—infinitude
cannot be touched.

Where breath slips—
the vine's hewn lot
remains. Absence—

one profiled face hangs
atop the flatness of another.
"But, can you see?"—

I am parted—
   I am past—

SOLITONS

Light—fog furrowing color, siphoning
deep hues, leaving thin-white
              on hollow fields, dead stalks

at dawn. Brackish light means with yellow. Light bleeds yellow
        through leaves like skin)(
                                this tree. Singular, the morning
ornate, precise precise (veins limbs roots) branching. We are

        rolling. The blue swatch, through

              the forking black
branches is (the figure)
curves
        flattening with
momentum (the ardor) of air (o slight slight

breeze) nearing lines, the successive
        shuffling—we've learned to name
invigorate, to name   heart-skip. Fish jump—
        it breaks the pattern
                                flattening curves,

        it is that the jumping has meaning, has
heaviness. The body wanting
        to feel sun (uncomfortable) flipping
slapping the blue, frenzied and furied. *How would you rise?*—

the ardor

        the long goose wings, bent as if elbows. Mysterious

flexors. We take it all for—the mechanics of wing—bones
        light enough to fly, change speed, drop
quick as fish jump. *How would you lower yourself? How would you*

rise?

                    *

I would have to reproduce the figure (again). Awkward
    flippant arrow, when I want to bend in. I would need someone
        to steady my hand. I would need someone to move me
through the stroke. I would want it,
           if my hand knew this, if
there were a track, a rut, a trammel, or
                    something—
some (necessary) leading to—
        the explanation adorned with a name, hackneyed
    hackneyed crocus bud,

named—

                    *

                  leaning—

everyone's name for the blackened autumn leaves, hanging
        dead from a limb—black bats sleeping or empty
bodies gathered or sculpted fragility (yes)—will you crumble
        and fall away? Because at the end there must be—

    but solitude freezes
in front of the stolid
door—
      if it were cracked, a bit
further? If the light poured all the way through?

        Could we see it?
        (Named: hands).

Who finds contentment with a name
    for the place no one would name? *Would you*
sit there? Would you   sit below the bridge? (see this?) lean
    on the tree, while bark pulls
at your skin, and hear this? Would you think of—

I can never never know—

the stolid)(the doorknob) *would you*
                                        reach; alter
     the angle, let more light in, would you look? Ponder
an end (because
                              there must be)—

that moves (you). What is the name
     of the moving? Which pheromone propels
the spider's bark-like body?

                                        * * *

Here is the corner, o burnt burnt
     field—flat, after the bank's slow descent.
Burnt (at dusk) without a name. The mind
          at the beginning, again, arduously
inching

          forward—but some of the grass dead, now,
and rolled over, as if beaten by a flood or
     blown—
a torrent. But, *slight, slight*

                    are you moved?

     I could sketch the sound in lines, but your question persists—*how
          does it move?* A small shifting
in the grass. A rising pitch hanging evenly above
     dried stalks. Others, shorter, higher. These spring up
quick—

these were two curves
                    flipped, points of bisection
connecting, back to (curved)
     back, touched and repelled, spilling—
flitting. The first

steadiness breaks. Comes back. And the shuffling
of sounds progressed (with ardor). Because
                    at the end there must be—
alighting. The white moth
                rises and falls, settles

among sticks—slow wings
                    precise wings—
obsequious chalky white and faint gray, small
        lime circle on the wing of
necessary. *Is it difficult to ascend?* I can never—

understand dusk. Pieces
        black, pieces glittering, green.
                            Dusk is a falling, a finishing
when angles retract. And shadows,

                            *

shadows are objects
        between the sun and the eye (no ardor). Do you see
these strips? *Would you* open the door—further? Would you notice
                    the lines glistening, the lines as silk
connecting the ends of grass? Would you lower yourself

to see?
    This plane
(it) needs
eye-level, it means
There must be

                            *

We had held fishing line between our fingers
        moved forward, moved
            back, until we understood
variety
        of pitch, of sound. We cannot

move back.
We have come this far, ebbing
     finery of thread, unnamable material
(of line) like silk,
             too—

It is what (necessarily)

            we cannot know

like the shadows, lengthening

    at dusk, like the fingers (of the hand)

stretching

reaching

toward

Two

NOTE: 19 OCTOBER

*

Unfurl my brow (my
hackneyed me) with dull
water, weak wind.

The storms (we want
to tie the mind) scatter
driftwood (we want

to know the tides)
wash the stilted house
away (to keep the body

full). The wetted walls
fill. They fall. And
desiccation wants

to keep (the body
with whispered things)
to sieve the tempest

thin, to furrow out
tinctured shells
uncover buries spirals

and inside one—
    one—

NOTE: 20 NOVEMBER

*

Pry the rust-worn
hinge apart (suffer
my cipher) let light

not splinter, let it
bleed (corundum-
hard-heart) blear

white. Flood
my wooden room
bluing it. (Slow

my tongue, slow
my speech) gentle feet
seek—risen

rings, split line—
a surface (no literal
temple, no literal

light) of wood.
Emptiness seeks
steps—*a knob.*

NOTE: 01 DECEMBER

*

Blanch the seeking
merchant's lost pearl
of gray—leave it

untouched, white.
Wear his list
pressed dark in

feathery paper.
Use water. Sallow
pools part the letters'

lines, take away
centers (unlatch
each step).

Unclip each wing
(for what will last?)
unshoe the horse—

use faith (the nacre of
the pearl will stick) to
tread the dust

without sound—
and ceaselessly—

NOTE: 03 JANUARY

*

No stones
to see. Seven
years. No iron.

No axe. To frieze
a sanctuary—soft
gold. Olivewood.

Cherubim wings.
Five cubits, one.
Two bodies hold

length (know ye—
the temple?) touching.
Four carved gourds,

palm trees, open
flowers in cedar walls.
No sound. (Hear ye—)

No earth inside. Air
molecules, rind-like, hold
hollowed yellow glare.

Out of darkness—
    Into it—

THREE

THE SPACE BETWEEN

There is the density of the crowd.

It doesn't matter which way the tourists are told
    to go: inside them you become them.
The answer is: we don't know which horror is correct.
    The moment has begun as a spring.

The people are leaning in.

In my mind, Barcelona is a row of green trees, a funnel
    to the labyrinth, leading down to the sea.
A man worries over a woman drinking alone, over a woman
    anxious to finally be alone.

It's Sunday and the church is packed.

I met one to escape the other. Mainly, we remember
    the flame; the arms thick
with pointing. Restricted to the surface the architecture
    is passing us by.

The leaves are red, are green, are gone.

In the dream I locked my jaw. It is real, though: everything
    has been enlarged. The burning. Mass
has eliminated the part of worry that can be touched. The man
    sits close to catch the woman's eye.

Mainly, we don't forget the flame: its quelling.

There is the density of destruction.

The building in Barcelona was burning. I remember the day
    only in pictures. There is a certain horror: now
people are descending. In Vienna, there is a grocery store under
    the ground, there is the opera only meters away.

The preacher's words keep moving.

The water was like whips, but compared to the flame: silent.
    The women buying *semmeln* will later go to the opera.
The man who designed the opera took his life, because it wasn't grand
    enough. The arms are still pointing and thick.

The leaves are red, are green, are gone.

The situation presented itself: to know each other deeper. The day
    that disappeared at the sea goes on, louder
than the dream. There is impossibility in this, if voiding
    means burning. If time could be straight.

It's Sunday and the church is packed.

The Viennese women wear dresses made to deeply touch skin.
    The opera is over. They walk home watching themselves
in darkened shop windows. The mind leaves itself
    on the street. The horror. We wouldn't waste it.

We watched the building burn into the ground.

There is the density of the house next door.

Describing this may be more difficult. Down our dining room table,
    like a stripe, in odd-shaped vases,
there is a row of tiny spring flowers. If this is an experiment,
    I like this. Am left with it. Need it.

The people keep leaning in.

I dream of summer feet on hardwood floors. Next door, figures
    cluttered on the mantel, shoes muck the back hall
closet. The man buys the woman a book to watch a woman writing.
    There is some need. The burning horror of a dream.

It's Sunday and the church is packed.

We have forgotten the expectations; the hollow sound we moved to
    as children. The shards are crossing,
like frantic spotlights. The memory was such that no one
    could write it down: our senses got lost there.

The leaves are red, are green, are gone.

Remember the building was burning. No, houses are burning, too.
                      Here, I mean.
    You still don't understand? The old Hungarian woman has a part
                    of the city step,
hanging, making an L with her cane. She is still hanging.
    The burnt hole in the roof of the first house, brings us
              the abundance of the next.

And the next day brought the first pile of shreds.

STRING THEORY

One (what [looms] field) in two—

If we understood
    the city through the window on the hill, it stood for something
we could hold. It reminds you—
                      descending was lengthy
the path mostly flat. We could not help to stop, to study the locks—
    to watch them segment the breathing, undo (mute mouth

    what tempts?) the yearning and afterwards
shut the gate, lock the city, where sound rolls—
    the baths' reptilian green, the baths' archaic wall (what word:
parts?) and water as one. But we did not understand—
    because where the sidewalk cracks, division

furthers. Veracity, counting dimensions, adding one for time. Lurking
    persists. No—time is woven, even if
the shadows move, even if shadows lurk, even if
    the object can throw its own complexity down, the shadow
is whole, can't shatter (hollow moon: we beseech).

We cannot keep the palpability, even if we sheave
    perceptions—because (we are endless) looking for this place
in our hands. We cannot. There in only one
    piece that will slip (What field:
looms?) our theory.

Two (hollow [beseech-ing] moon) in three—

Leaving and watching, we are waving, charting
a hand to fingers to speck to dust. What will return to me
    if I trust? (Mute mouth: what word) Descending is—
the alphabet—we think we crave
                    repetition. It reminds us—

we cannot. This verticality is woven, beseech. But gravity—
    the polar too close. The air too thick. (Hollow moon:
what field)(What part: tempts) Seek we
                    stomata. The dimensions
are curled away. We cannot—

    see. The sheet, flapping. The lower-cased
gods, purling the street. And quixotic (what part
    tempts) the words, they roll
                away. (What beseech:
looms?)

If I lean against the wall, will it move? Will it speak,
    if I lean? Will you tell the sheaf of worn letters
to pick itself up? I cannot. I need the vertical falling, this rain—
    this drenching halt. I need holographic proof. Missing dimension—
descend. Find wind. Find rain. Touch the featureless drops.

              And three

                    (what [parts] word) in four

              And four

                    (mute [what] mouth) in five

              And five

BLUEPRINTS

The woman wants a painting of one hill.

Outside, day stained dusk—too darkly
      blue. The moon's uneven press, a graft.

We consider it in each of the rooms.

    The dangling fish, scaled languor
spilling (cold chain

        coiling) heavy in my palm. Now, I must

keep the bead suspended
    in bright fluid between black lines.

The first room was lighter than this. Balanced—

      trodden-green on gray-
blue. Each of us agrees.

    We inhabit the cavernous.

I am the blind man and cannot recognize
    steep grade, nor hear bent legs toil.

I think fields spill at the ends—

    color and cloth and curves, a frame holding
standing the hill up—straight.

                         * * *

Given a skyline, build—want

a lasting—fearlessness. No earthquake, no
      consideration of stress. He raises the dome without

centering. (The records now faded and in Latin.)

      Did Brunelleschi know other domes
of brick? The arduous task of covering. Of skin?

     Each fish brings with it a sea.

Horizontally, one arch supports the next.
      Quarter widths touch, three quarters

free. Each stone fraught. *Remember*—

     No center for support. If I carve,
can I see—

      How long is composition?

I feel the city standing before the ruin
      before the risen dome breaks

the line of fog; octagonal

     shells, herringbone bonds, the drum,
nine rings of horizontal arches, dovetail stone.

               * * *

   But I saw no temple in it . . .

This canopy is pine, loose weave
      of reed and airy. *And the city had no need*

of the sun or of the moon

   to shine in it. Shuffled dimensions
confuse—

where else have I stood

intersecting rows? Splotches shifting
    the sky. Angles, pulling in—

Slowly,

       I wander to a center. Drawn. Eye-level, branches
whorl, spoke-like, lopped off—extend and extend

    only the body the interstice—

caught. Needles on the sky, still
      green. The bundled

pine caught on

    branches, unevenly aligned, wish-
bone spaces opening to my feet—asking.

* * *

    This fish *is* dead on the dock—

body open, head attached to one half. Obdurate
      scales oppose the run of wood—standing

thinned portions on end. Protruding

    the mandible holds the convex eye (the fish's furthest
reach) glassed-over, completely black, from pressing in.

    Not limp, nor flat. This body is structured.

Fins, caudal and dorsal, hold lake water
    together in teary drops. Heavy, on wet fins—it leaks

it nails the fullness of the body to the slowly buckling dock.

The bright flesh soaks sun, intensifies
color for a translucent fish spine.

Who carved this space? It reminds us

the ribs much thinner than needles of pine. Would you
lift the inner structure out? (Have you

peeled back fish skin, draped it

re-skinning muscles lining your hand?) Would the pinned
ribs sink back? Are they buoyant, light enough to—

FOUR

MECHANICS

The truss cuts early Autumn's blue plane
    into uneven strips. Loss—
merging
color, darkness into this
                    widening line, this blurred

frame. It holds, but the holding heavy
the frame not straight. We can never
touch the trusses. (They are a strong math.) Though
                                     I do not doubt.

The leaves are (still) green. Fish still slip
    especially in the fishhouse
                           the eye (still) stares
on the bed of crushed ice.

    Is this a need (for interruption)?

(And) the frame is not
    straight (and) the car moves on (and)
the mind goes back (and) the hand
                    still waves.

    Learning to find the moment, she said, is something solid

we can build ourselves on. The moment

(I know) is not, it is
                    the division of water, seeing this once
or: I will forget my eyes and see the thing doubled. I need
                                to understand

(the mind is divided, but) the passing
                       we never see.
What is (need)
        watching?

Consider that the car moves at an average speed.
The river is the Rappahannock
                              and cantilevers hold us (here).
The town behind us empties out. Small houses (I do not know—

what is their name?) fall from the center, teeter
in a nervous line. Trailers grid the top of the bank.
The whitewash of the fishing boat (below) reflects

noon's straight glare. But (I want)
to touch the wood. Each existence
extends. It is precarious

or: it grows—it moves
forward (from edge to bank
with fish) with the straight

                         truss and time. Speak or hear—
There are two halves.
This part is not involved.

Units of words/mystery/faulting/folding/the history of calling

What is it we cannot see?

And how then shall we begin?

The moment necessary for crossing—
     it is not easy
to find. I know nothing about physics,
     mystery is finding each moment, struggling—
each axis—every point.

The man, below, reels in the fish, holds
     its fat body in his bare hands, stopping
the struggle, stilling it, lifting it
     off the hook—there is a hole
(now) below the fish's lip

but the fish still slips. We keep supposing
moving depends on this. The shadows
    of the trusses (now) cut the sun into strips.

And consciousness—named (mind)

                                        (named) space?

Now whitecaps, because wind. Shadows faster
    and less and less sun. Or:

Which pieces would you choose to carry over?

I was standing in the middle
                                of the hill (the voice (still)
                                        stands). The eyes looked
with persuasion. I turned
                    (missed ascent) did not achieve—
                                the eyes too full (the voice)

    too heavy.

The view best from the top? I will never—

(see)/fingers/figures/penciled/paper
with grids. The grids for keeping
the lead in straight lines. The arrows (also)

arcs of precision, and rows upon rows and pages.
To stack the pale green grids, to hold them
in my hand. The grid for the numbers—

for the safety of line. Memory—
                            I will cross
                                the bridge. The words—
move around the room.

    Live crabs
                in summer. Raw oysters
    in Autumn—their gray mass (in)
                            a punch bowl (and)

the small cup holds almost

      twelve two-tined forks.

Brazil nuts fall, triangular (from)

       the shell. The shell

is empty. (It is)

    hollowed out. We can

know (touch)

    the inside. It is rough. (It is)

sculpted.

   Will you

     not come again?

   I will go—

there soon.

   Will you

     not come again?

   I will cross—

the river twice

    (The fishing boats are gone

      the water is strange and gray.

    She sits inside and stares

      at rough pages of a book.

    She moves her fingers

      down the margins

    thinks of empty space

      names the space)

the bridge.

MORPHOLOGY

I

Not the listing of flowers, but quivering—
    the outstretched hand. A mass of weedy
flowers bunched and breaking

    from the fist. Marmoreal, her hand.
These colors faintly hint. A method
    of stepping, passing. Stillness starts

the need—staccato frantic force
    'tis in my memory locked—the need
lulls. I begin

    unabashed and doubt and search am drawn
shaking a foot lurching (denting stems) stepping—
    Folding segment (of stair) when will you end?

The dream was a ladder (mine, too). Each flight
    moves up or down. The understanding lost
and pieces and flight and who is it—

    coming down? Rewriting
the letter (again and again) tracing
    the madness (desire)

(moves through) to need. Rearranging. I face
    the empty room—first a (simple) chair,
face the empty room—first (unfinish) the floor.

    My road turned (to empty). *Do you doubt
that?* Constant, this (locking) need to offer—
A table, a room, a flower—one step

The space of a church is the space of a church.
I have been   affrighted   needed her
words   (here)   needed   an order
to see.   To touch.
                    Eyes (they) *bended their light on me.*
And room   bent   cannot be
        but seep   (the words)
from hollow.   What is the length of a space?
Will my hand reach the next rung?   I am half-
way.   Who is coming   toward   me?
seemed to find his way without his eyes.   I am
a mason. I am   not proud. I am   standing
        on the stoop of a twelfth-century church.
If I reach   will it prolong   the chain
        of voice of words of lifting. But words
(I hold) are brick   and heavy.

Drawn to the intricate letter, slowness
    of my hand. Strokes slow, strokes
dark. A filling. Without space (I knew)
    the inability of breath. *I think nothing,*
need—

Do you consider breath an arc?

The woman stands by the grave
    and calls. *A noble mind here*
overthrown. The edge of slow (her need)
    will quiver. It does not mean
death. The living ekes. And we are so caught

in fright. Will the pieces (still) fit?

Could the call be complete? The rain had stopped.
    We spend the morning bailing out our boat.
The walls are wood. We step
    the boat lowers and water will rise.
We begin to understand—parting, the fog, thick.

Do you believe in interruption, segmenting a list?

The loon's dense black body
    mimics the sunken hull of the boat. The walls
are wood. The loon dives deep. But we cannot
    catch the fog, cannot learn to keep
it in our hands. To offer. And does desire move?

Could beauty have better commerce than with honesty?

The loon's cry echoes from the wooden plane of the lake,
    pushes through fog. There is an unknown. I am so a-
part. The fog, the loon, the boat. The shore
    drifts away. The pieces are sacred. And the loon
dives (deep). *O woe is me, T' have seen*—to breathe.

I did not believe the voice would float.

Vision brings the pieces back in frames. Each sacredness is a dilapidated house. *Great blue heron* on Carter's Creek. It shifts stillness. *Chestnut-backed chickadee*. I—fear—is—vision—of—I would—tear—just one wall— unfinish the floor. Sacred. (The offering) Wing-space. (neither up nor down)? What is it lies beneath this wall? *Great blue heron*, folds of neck, the S. Silence is—quick. *Osprey*. Why do they number the nests? *Osprey*. The numbers are consuming the creek. We have been wrong for so long. Watch *great blue heron*. Remember, I have touched the hidden side of brick. The time is past.

5

stone marked

rushing Linn

it interrupt-

ed space she'

d have called

FIVE

NOTE: 15 MARCH

*

At Winter's cusped end
seven silver leaves
hang. Coruscant

in crevices (my close
eye) caught shine—
seven silvered cocoons

heavy. Silk still wound
on tight red, tight
wrapped bark. (What new

heaven?) A vivisection—
my rare bride (red
tawny yellow, beryl

green) enveloped.
Too fast the saplings
bud (my measure

spent—my rod).
The swollen centers
plead. Let nothing

unopened—
        nothing—

NOTE: 03 APRIL

*

Mid-morning's wrens
wrap my house (frantic
fealty) in chords of flight

ephemeral—voiced.
Branched things (I
stretched too far) forgot

cotyledon-green. Winter's
wizened leaf (disintegration,
stains) abandoned—

a body. Pieces of
death (not once, not
twenty times) gathered—

a living. Sides of salt (I
did not find the edge of
grain) unmeasured.

What to preserve? Bent
bones clench. Snow drifts
drifts melt. Thick mist.

NOTE: 04 APRIL

*

And farm machinery
on flatbed trucks. Not rural.
Not urban. Heaviness is—

what thinking thing is held
inside my skin? (What distance
is—) The dying

leaf dust catches in folds—
my hand. (Adamantine—
my prayer.) The flat

shell rendered still (what
beached life—) covers
the fractional

sand (asking—
oblique). And distance is—
that shallow thing (I

lift). Skip it. Then
watch each small splash
time marked in jumps—

how stitched—
        I am—

NOTE: 20 MAY

*

Through tight glass
tarnished thimbles—
the checkered score

steel-flattened domes—
oblate (not yet
pierced). To my eyes

dust sticks. (What—
to spare me?) Choose
one. Take off-beat

claves—the sheathing
wild—it wraps Spring
buds (forgive me—)

in wilted thread. Wind
rolls tall grass—
presses (I've torn

the newly branched
away) bright sheen
on the flat. What looks

thin, full—
and inside—

NOTE: 2 5 MAY

*

Bellowing—runged cry (here
the church) teeters without
precision. Here—compass

arms press themselves
(I am watching doors
slam) with wind—

so that in turning—tearing
sounds dissolve (here
the steeple). A ladder

measures my ascent.
Numbered breath (open
what door?) calls

confused directions—
out. Each dusk our house
splits (halved shadow halved

light). The ascension
dream—slow. (Now, open
the door). *Count—*

NOTE: 21 JUNE

*

The fabric
full—the jar
filling

night's frame
in languish—
a box (show

thy self—) one
swallow feather
(take me) three

stones (make me—
the path).
Pinioned, I

am flooded. I
am full. Grown
heavy. Memory

folds objects—
What remains—
we ask—

NOTE: 22 JUNE

*

No skin on skin, nor face
against another
face. My firmament

a house. Watching
doors in windows, oceans
through (open) doors. Faith

rote on me. Impalpable
wind mass—lifting
broken sea grass

stretching shadows
strewing my path. These
walls are thick—

my house—heavy.
The peninsula leans
away. No shadow

can return. Flatly,
speak it. Write it
in my eye. I am by faith

winnowed—
    I am weed—

NOTE: 01 JULY

*

The ocean's wide
roughness risks—gathers
in my closed fist

tight womb (tight
me) curled in. Salt-
stained pebbles

stir—revenant
(flattening out my
palm) it lifts. Can I

chip my voice out—let it
drop one by one? You
shut the sea—closed it

in doors (stilled grief
folds in). The shell's
enameled slope draws

back—I cannot see.
What ascension
in things? I ask

full feet—
    let me flee—

Six

NOTE: 30 AUGUST

*

Easier for flooded fields
to plead (listen to me
in silence) vitality.

In stagnant pools
the rows (hide me
in the shadows) admit

vacuity. The mirrored
levitation breaks
math (the burgeoning

man's made) one
ragged cloth laid
flat. And how

are the swatches
stitched? Closely
do you hear?

Little risings—each
effervescence lifts.
Blown willow—

show me—

NOTE: 02 SEPTEMBER

*

Late afternoon's angled
glare (sidelong—one
desire) brushes

shell ends—thinly
the shadows drape
sand in crescent

shapes (an aggregate—
unskeined). Peeled back
boundary (what distance

between two sides
of line?) naming waves'
(tight, rifting) speed—

departure time (we are
watching) a yellowing
foam (the lightness

of) the seen part of (I
think) disintegration—
what is left—

All yesterday—
    All today—

NOTE: 03 SEPTEMBER

*

Inenarrable—shifts in-
side the sea (conglomerate
tesserae) etch dark

shapes. Contour (us
thinking) the flattened
ocean floor—shunting

shadows (can I name
our hovering?)—bodies
amoebic—black-cast

and blown—unveiling
quick stipple-light (un-
known). Beginnings

in wet cloth—a billowing
carves choice (a new-caved
thing)—reifies weight.

Is blown. Silence—
implored. I clench on.
Wrung salt drips.

NOTE: 31 SEPTEMBER

*

Let my cloth more
bare (threadbare
me) untie each knot.

Let bent shine
in sequins fall. (Listen—
light taps tile floor)

light loops
gathering (give me
thinned words) a pile

one coarse gown (Listen—
straighten me) one woolen
weight, one careless weave.

Knit me—

One star, one pearl
(Listen—of what
am I made?)

ask me—

NOTE: 07 OCTOBER

*

Night's feeble
end (count me
undone) still

burns. And morning
wind cannot hold it
here. Unintelligible

wings on wind—
cutting grave streaks
for the shuffling

sky. (What piece
must fall?) My hands,
stones. Adding—

giving sound to
a quick stream's
silent running.

Stop me. Use
wet moth wings.
Slow me—

NOTE: 12 NOVEMBER

*

Dye me—indigo,
cobalt, carmine.
No. Choose one

more bound to bleed
—might stain my life
longer—might

keep in my skin.
Summer's closing
petals (come out

come out) plead
hang, wilt, go
black. (Do not hide—

from me.)(Come.)
Give me an edge—
cliff the fields—

dangle my legs—
swell my feet—
make each step—

help me—
        harder—

NOTE: 12 NOVEMBER

*

And ossify my slow
lament. I broke.
Am broken. False

panicle, what does
spread out? The body
dulled, gone blank.

Salt burns, seals
my both eyes
shut. (Loved—

what?)
　　　(Return—
bones.) Shadow,

come. Pass
one hand through me—
again, bowed neck,

odd prayer—
shadowed wrist—
inside me. Closeness

came. Once—
　　It is gone—

NOTE: 12 NOVEMBER

*

Touch-me-not,
what have you burnt
with orange—what

can you keep?
Seed-shaped black
small streaks—cinch

me shut. One piece.
A broken lock.
One piece. Prayer—

small words. Broken
plea. What keeps
the petal tongued

together? Dried
it longs. Open *this*
lock. To split.

Please dampen.
Please. How else
I beg? Red flame—

spread it flat—
release—

SEVEN

MIGRATION

The series has been reduced to one bad sketch,
the rectangular frame of which is five lines.
         They misconnect. The ground is the horizon
is a line, three-quarters the width of the frame.
         And though the sodden field is spelt in small
dips—where the insects invisibly live,
         the picture will not hint at the reason. It
is a gnatting mass of dots, and of the two
         lower, looking closer to dashes, and these
are the birds that drop—these are the reason
         for the sketching (I have added an arrow

to indicate wind). The wind had been blowing,
         remember: the wings barely moved. The storm
left. To think that the storm always leaves again.
         And the two birds re-tangle themselves, inside
the skein. It is endocytotic—It
         has to be, to keep closeness with the body's
uncanny math. That ghost in me. That blown net,
         a gate at the base of the mouth, unsheathing
words, turning them to speech. Assuring some things.
         Explaining this sketch, or that, once again, all
the storms we have known will go away. But why

         is the horizon smaller than the frame? What
is this impulse to shorten things? The series
         was meant to lead us somewhere. To consider
children stirring up silt in a puddle, and
         the puddle nimming the cloud for its face, and
the nimbus belonging to an abstract need,
         a desire, and how, undoubtedly, this
would, also, rise—how it rises, even,
         in the monks' lithe chants, how it gets stronger in
the density of unfamiliar words, and
         the tin bell sound breaking incense smoke, wafting

down to us, in bits, softening, giving the sound
                an edge. And beauty *is* thickness, how it bends.
This series was meant to be a wish. Thinking,
        if two birds fall, or if speech rises up, from
an unseen place to what is—then I might,
                finally, be stone. Sculpted and placed. Will you
remember the pietà? The day spent
        watching it, how certain it seemed to be small.
You would let me keep my eyes, that I might look
                forever. *This* could be assurance. I would
never move. I promise. Will never move.

THE VENATION OF A FRENATE

If sorrow only nets a tomb, then steep my eyes, then split the twine.

The mourning man, he shifts his weight, turns the prayer, sending it down

(and pilgrim and kite and pine)

and begs with bent arrows and stones, like lithic knells could loose the ground.
He screws the prayer to send it down.

No still-water, no eludent gaze—come eddy, keep me—closed

like lithic knells will loose hard ground.

The ancient chamber fills with sand, our house is going, toll on toll.
Come eddy, now, and keep me—close.

Come brace the woman full with fear. She's shaking the door, blocks in her eyes.
Our house is gone. We toll, we woe.

And only the bolt, gone full with black. The bolt to mark the latching line,

not shaking the door and blocks in your eyes,

no furious try, no object to count—go out, go in. I cannot remain.
No bolt to mark my latching line,

no coaxing, no calling (*cannot*) but balsa on balsa, my sticking frame.
Go out. Go out. I won't remain.

Do you see the field's even splay? The Monarchs' wings flatly tack, but balsa on balsa my sticking frame.

Each solid edge can fray in time, like goldenrod gone brown, long past,

but Monarchs' wings, flatly tack.

We try to hold our vision here. We bleach the color to trace the veins,

like goldenrod gone brown, long past,

like windows, glass on glass; to press the wings to bleed the stain,

bleach the color to trace the veins. Then steep my eyes to split the twine,

keep pressing the wings to bleed the stain. And pilgrim. And kite. And pine.

BLACK AND WHITE OR RED AND BLUE

It was acceptable not to understand,
there are always acute biologies,
frenzied projects—crazed birds inverting (roiled
images) their parabolic flight; words
moving anger down the page like a track,
untangling (again, birds) our silent sky,
        but the accusation—
falling into
states of (un)consciousness, undoing words.
The never-ending phone call repeating
death. Of course, now you also want to hear
the voice. He says, *old-timey—the body-at-home-
in-the-house*. Of course, this makes you conscious
again of your teeth. Overlapping teeth,
touch-me-death. This happened before. The rain
an inexorable sentence, making
red leaves redder (driving it becomes worse)
black roads blacker, say miracle, broken
yellow fragments. Say *Corpus Callosum:*
a nerve conducting conduit—two halves.
Paint one gray. Look two fists. Now, paint one red.
We cannot be smart, it cannot be fair;
this body visaged; this visage coffered.
The dummy divided in half—show us
our choices. Driving is now creative
time. We value that droning inner voice.
I believe in the holy science of
this place, in the once and never the same
intricate folds, they are un-sculptable
wrinkles. Testify, for us, as our sole
evidence of tangible memory.
Here this untouchable woman, here
that voluptuous hag. Even cold floors
allude warm fur of rugged dog bellies,
the sporadic coos in rhetorical speech
call genetics (recognize: three sisters);

an insisting we know ourselves better.
        This is only an example—
slipping
loosing consciousness, like we learned before.
Driving. Missing funerals, there are other
appointments, other odes to fragility,
birds alone in the sky. When the time comes
the eye patch (*credo ut intelligam*)
remove it. She says you will see, again.

NOTES

Corymb   "*O my floating life*" is taken from Lorine Niedecker's "Paean to Place."

Solitons   The term *solitons* comes from the study of physics and is defined as solitary waves (as in a gaseous plasma) that retain their shape and speed after colliding with each other.

Note: *01 December*   In the second line, the merchant refers to Matthew 13.

Note: *03 January*   The temple referred to is Solomon's, as described in 1 Kings 6.

Blueprints   The second section is inspired by reading on Filippo Brunelleschi's construction of the dome of S. Maria del Fiore, particularly Rowland J. Mainstone's essay in *The Engineering of Medieval Cathedrals* and Giorgio Vasari's *Lives of Seventy Painters, Sculptors, and Architects.* In the third section, the italicized lines are from Revelation 21.

Mechanics   The term *moment* comes from the study of mechanics and is the momentum of a force around a specific point.

Morphology   The italicized lines in sections 1–3 are taken, accordingly, from Acts 1–3 of *Hamlet* and are spoken by Ophelia. In section 4, the italics are mine.

Note: *31 September*   "Knit me— // One Star, one pearl" refers to Henry Vaughan's "Distraction."